Published by Canon Press
P.O. Box 8729, Moscow, Idaho 83843
800.488.2034 | www.canonpress.com

Toby J. Sumpter, *Worldview Guide for Moby-Dick*
Copyright ©2017 by Toby J. Sumpter.
Cited page numbers come from the Canon Classics edition of the book (2016),
www.canonpress.com/books/canon-classics.

Cover design by James Engerbretson
Cover illustration by Forrest Dickison
Interior design by Valerie Anne Bost and James Engerbretson

Printed in the United States of America.

A free end-of-book test and answer key are available for download at
www.canonpress.com/ClassicsQuizzes

17 18 19 20 21 22   9 8 7 6 5 4 3 2 1

WORLDVIEW GUIDE

MOBY-DICK

Toby J. Sumpter

canonpress
Moscow, Idaho

CONTENTS

INTRODUCTION

"Call me Ishmael" is one of the most famous opening lines in all of literature. Intriguing, haunting, suggestive, ambiguous—the narrator does not say that his name is Ishmael. He summons the reader to call him by that name. And in so doing, the narrator invites the reader not merely into a story but an epic, a tale that encompasses life, death, the universe, God, angels, demons, and man caught in the eye of that cosmic hurricane. If you consent to call him Ishmael, you consent to this voyage.

THE WORLD AROUND

When *Moby-Dick* was first published in 1851 in three volumes, the young American republic was perhaps at its greatest blotto of romantic nationalism. With the cries of democracy and freedom of the press and worker's rights, the European revolutions of 1848 had churned out their bloody waves, and America likewise flexed its "Manifest Destiny" muscles. After the first wagon train set out on the Oregon Trail with over a thousand pioneers in tow in 1843, America took full possession of the Oregon Territories south of the 49th parallel in 1846. In 1848, the Mexican-American War secured possession of Texas and what would become a number of other western states including California, making America a transcontinental nation, stretching from the Atlantic all the way to the Pacific Ocean.

The first telegraph message had been sent by Samuel Morse from Baltimore to Washington D.C. in 1844, and by 1851, there was a telegraph line between London and Paris. Isaac Singer had patented the first sewing machine, Millard Fillmore was the 13th president of the United States, Nathaniel Hawthorne's *The Scarlet Letter* was hot off the presses, and Harriet Beecher Stowe had begun stirring up the abolitionist movement with her installments of *Uncle Tom's Cabin*.

The Second Great Awakening had largely subsided, but not before Brigham Young had led 148 Mormon converts out to the Salt Lake Valley in 1847, and arguably, much of the passionate religious fervor that remained merely shifted its focus outward into the massive social, economic, and political spheres, churning with more foam and muddy current as the decade wore on, drifting ultimately to Civil War.

ABOUT THE AUTHOR

Herman Melville was born on August 1, 1819, the grandson of two celebrated Revolutionary War veterans. He was the third child of his father Allen Melville, an optimistic but reckless businessman who spent much of Herman's youth traveling, trying to make his fortune.

Allen appears to have assumed his father's Unitarianism. Herman's mother was Maria Gansevoort Melville who was raised in a devout Dutch Reformed family, and she supplied Herman with his vast biblical knowledge. Herman's father died in 1832, and after a short stint in school, in the spring of 1839, Herman made arrangements to sail on a merchant ship as a cabin boy from New York to Liverpool, England.

There is little information to go on after that point, but judging from his semi-autobiographical novels that began appearing after 1845, it appears that Melville spent those years at sea and in various exotic locations related to his travels. He married Elizabeth Shaw around 1847 after the successes of his first two novels. *Moby-Dick* was then published in 1851 to mixed reviews, and after his novel *Pierre* was not received very well in 1852, Melville began writing short fiction and later poetry. He took a job as a customs inspector for a number of years to pay the bills, and didn't write another novel until *Billy Budd* at the very end of his life, which was left unfinished when he died on September 27, 1891.

WHAT OTHER NOTABLES SAID

"He is very backward in speech & somewhat slow in comprehension, but you will find him as far as he understands men & things both solid & profound, & of a docile & amiable disposition."
~ Allen Melville (Melville's father, about young Herman, age 7)

"Not in his subject alone, but in his style is Melville distinctively American. It is large in idea, expansive; it has an Elizabethan force and freshness and swing, and is, perhaps, more rich in figures than any style but Emerson's. It has the picturesqueness of the new world, and, above all, a free-flowing humour, which is the distinct cachet of American literature."
~ Archibald MacMechan, c. 1899

"I think that the book which I put down with the unqualified thought 'I wish I had written that' is *Moby-Dick*. The Greek-like simplicity of it: a man

of forceful character driven by his somber nature
and his bleak heritage, bent on his own destruction and dragging his immediate world down with
him with a despotic and utter disregard of them
as individuals; the fine point to which the various natures caught (and passive as though with a
foreknowledge of unalterable doom) in the fatality
of his blind course are swept—a sort of Golgotha
of the heart become immutable as bronze in the
sonority of its plunging ruin; all against the grave
and tragic rhythm of the earth in its most timeless
phase: the sea. And the symbol of their doom: a
White Whale."

~ William Faulkner, c. 1927

SETTING, CHARACTERS, AND PLOT SUMMARY

Ishmael is the young sailor and narrator who, finding himself "growing grim about the mouth" with a "damp, drizzly November" in his soul, decides it's high time to get to sea as soon as possible (1).[1] Making his way to New Bedford on the coast of Massachusetts, he takes lodging at the Spouter-Inn and becomes the bedfellow of one pagan, head-pedaling islander prince named Queequeg, who for "all his tattooings was on the whole a clean, comely looking cannibal" (27).

Becoming fast friends, Ishmael and Queequeg sail out to the famous whaling island of Nantucket, thirty miles off the coast of Massachusetts. They sign up with Captains Bildad and Peleg, "Quakers with a vengeance" (85), who happen to be the joint owners and agents of the *Pequod*, a

---

1. All page numbers reference the Canon Classics edition of *Moby-Dick* (Moscow, ID: Canon Press, 2016).

whaling ship to be commanded by the darkly mysterious, one-legged Captain Ahab. The *Pequod* leaves the Nantucket harbor on Christmas Day, but not before Ishmael and Queequeg are severely warned that their journey on the *Pequod* can only end in disaster by an old beggar man named Elijah.

Starbuck is the chief mate on the *Pequod*, a native of Nantucket and a Quaker by descent, a thin but hardened and courageous man. Stubb is the second mate, from Cape Cod, the "whistling tinker," good humored, with a pipe as "one of the regular features of his face" (136–7). Flask is the third mate, a native of Tisbury in Martha's Vineyard, a short, stout, ruddy, young fellow. These three are the headsmen of the three whaling boats. Queequeg is the harpooner in Starbuck's boat. Tashtego is an Indian from Gay Head in Martha's Vineyard and is the harpooner in Stubb's boat. Ahasuerus Daggoo is a giant black man, an African "savage" standing at six foot five inches with two golden hoops in his ears "so large that the sailors called them ring-bolts, and would talk of securing the top-sail halyards to them" (139). Daggoo is the harpooner for Flask. Finally, there is Pip, the little black boy from Alabama.

While the *Pequod* is in theory bound for whaling grounds wherever they might be found, Captain Ahab makes it clear to the ship's crew that there is really only one, burning, all-consuming aim on this voyage: "Whosoever of ye raises me a white-headed whale with a wrinkled brow and a crooked jaw; whosoever of ye raises me that white-headed whale, with three holes punctured in his starboard fluke—look ye, whosoever of ye raises me that same white whale, he shall have this gold ounce, my boys!" (189). In this famous scene, Captain Ahab nails a sixteen-dollar gold piece to the mast and announces the quest to seek Moby Dick. It was that white whale that "dismasted" Ahab, taking off his leg, and Ahab swears that he'll "chase him round Good Hope, and round the Horn, and round the Norway Maelstrom, and round per-dition's flames" before he gives him up (190). While Star-buck, Stubb, and Flask balk at this mission of vengeance, Ahab calls upon the harpooners and crew to drink an oath that "God hunt us all, if we do not hunt Moby Dick to his death!" (195).

At the first lowering (to hunt a whale), a fourth whal-ing boat and crew suddenly emerges from the shadows, which Ahab commands himself with five other men of Asian or Middle Eastern descent, the harpooner being the white-turbaned old man named Fedallah. While the *Pequod* does indeed hunt whales and harvest them a-plenty in the months that follow in the Atlantic and Indian Oceans, the ship presses ever eastward toward the Pacific Ocean, the last known whereabouts of Moby Dick. The *Pequod* meets (gams) with nine other ships in total as it sails east, beginning with the *Jeroboam* whose captain pleads with Ahab to desist from his insane quest, culmi-nating in the *Delight*, "most miserably misnamed," a wreck of a ship, shattered and splintered by the very white whale they are seeking. The story culminates in a final, three-day chase, leaving only Ishmael alive to tell the tale.

WORLDVIEW ANALYSIS

Moby-Dick is a great and magnificent tragedy. Like the ocean liner *Titanic*, it soars with humanistic beauty, ingenuity, humor, understanding, a sense of dread and destiny, and yet it ultimately drives like a raging madman into the hard reality of the world God created. *Moby-Dick* is both an American epic and, as a literary genre, a romantic tragedy.

And yet, for somewhat obvious reasons, *Moby-Dick* is highly reminiscent of the biblical story of Jonah. It contains a man who seems to have gone mad at sea and is defeated by a whale, along with an argument, a struggle, a storm of words and emotions about what is right, what is good, and what is fair. The book of Jonah famously ends with God's unanswered question to Jonah, fuming and wishing to die. Is the story of Jonah, like *Moby Dick*, a romantic tragedy?

"In token of my admiration for his genius, this book is inscribed to Nathaniel Hawthorne." So reads Herman Melville's dedication of *Moby-Dick* to his friend and contemporary American author. Hawthorne, like Melville, remains one of the principal players in the American romantic project.

Of course, in order to make any sense of these claims, we need to define our terms. Romanticism is not the genre of cheap paperbacks at the grocery store. Rather, Romanticism is a current of thought, belief, life, and art characterized by the numinous, the mystical, the poetic, the emotions and feelings of humanity wrestling with the wild, beautiful, and ultimately tragic forces of nature, and behind all of that, even God Himself. Albert Camus, the 20th-century French philosopher wrote this about *Moby-Dick* and several other Melville titles: "These anguished books in which man is overwhelmed, but in which life is exalted on each page, are inexhaustible sources of strength and pity. We find in them revolt and acceptance, unconquerable and endless love, the passion for beauty, language of the highest order—in short, genius."[2] Anguish, love, strength, pity, passion for beauty, and the exaltation of life—all of these are characteristics of the Romantics.

These sensibilities are evidenced in the breadth and depth of *Moby-Dick's* subject matter and language. On

---

2. Andrew Delbanco, *Melville: His World and Work* (New York: Vintage Books, 2013), xiv.

the surface, it is the story of a mad whaling captain set on revenge, but if that's what you're hoping for, you will be deeply disappointed. Melville expands his subject matter far beyond this slender plot line. This is because, for the Romantic, nothing in this world is so simple, so plain, so mundane. The Romantic sees in a masthead the history of the world, life, death, beauty, and God. Oceans, men, and stars pulse with glory and divinity. And perhaps most mysteriously in this particular novel, it is the sea monster, the leviathan, the great white sperm whale that is the constant nagging curiosity, wonder, terror, fury, even love.

Moby-Dick is about men who go to sea, about ships and sailors and sails, about ropes and harpoons and storms at sea, about eating and sleeping on a whale ship, about the meaning of whales, stories of whales, pictures of whales, fossils of whales, the biology and physiology of whales, about killing and harvesting whales.

The thing to understand chiefly about Romanticism is that it is fundamentally a worldview of despair. But as men are not inclined to live out their assumptions consistently, they tend to dress their despair up in their finest drag. Paul says that unrighteous man naturally tends to suppress the truth: "For what can be known about God is plain to them, because God has shown it to them … so they are without excuse. For although they knew God, they did not honor him as God or give thanks to him, but they became futile in their thinking, and their foolish hearts were darkened. Claiming to be wise, they became fools, and exchanged the glory of the immortal God for images resembling mortal man and birds and animals and creeping things" (Rom. 1:18–23).

Notice several things about this passage from Romans. First, what can be known about God is plain to all men but they suppress this truth. Second, they refuse to give God thanks or honor him as God, and in so doing, they become futile in their thinking and their foolish hearts are darkened. And finally, having become fools, they claim to be wise. Along with this comes an exchange of glory, and the clear implication is that the reason they exchange God's glory for other bits of created glory is because they have convinced themselves that it's better. This goes along with claiming to be wise. They would not claim to be wise and knowingly downgrade their glory.

This means that when a man or woman or a community or culture at large is in the process of turning away from the true God of heaven, they do so by suppressing the truth of God, refusing to honor Him and thank Him, and in their folly and darkened minds, they substitute another glory in place of God.

Now the point of all this is that Romanticism is one of those attempts to ignore God and replace His glory. This is why the language is soaring and majestic, why the subject matter is epic, transcendent, and philosophical. The Romantics are grasping for nothing less than divine glory, and yet with few exceptions, what is actually presented is

an "exchanged glory" done up in rouge and eye shadow—
the "glory" of tragedy covering over the despair. Melville,
whatever his personal convictions or beliefs, is clearly
caught up in that cultural fervor, and in this sense *Moby-Dick* is a breathtaking exhibit of what rebellious men
can make in their attempts to evade the God of heaven.

Listen to Melville rhapsodize:

> Men may seem detestable as joint stock companies
> and nations; knaves, fools, and murderers there
> may be; men may have mean and meager faces,
> but man, in the ideal, is so noble and so sparkling,
> such a grand and glowing creature, that over any
> ignominious blemish in him all his fellows should
> run to throw their costliest robes…. But this august
> dignity I treat of, is not the dignity of kings and
> robes, but that abounding dignity which has no
> robed investiture. Thou shalt see it shining in the
> arm that wields a pick or drives a spike; that demo-
> cratic dignity which, on all hands, radiates without
> end from God; Himself! The great God absolute!
> The center and circumference of all democracy! His
> omnipresence, our divine equality!" (134-5)

It's a passage like this that gives Melville away. He
wants a god made in the image of man, not man made in
the image of the true and living God. For all his biblical
allusions and citations, for all his appeals to God, Melville imagines a world that is hardly distinguishable from
pantheism—god is in all things and all things are in god.
The harpooners represent this pantheistic and godlike

nativism. Queequeg, Tashtego, Daggoo, and Fedallah represent that noble-savage, democratic dignity, uncorrupted by (Christian) civilization. What is hard to understand is that this so-called dignified vision of man is not merely false but is in fact deadly and dangerous. Read what Melville makes of America:

> We Americans are the peculiar, chosen people — the Israel of our time; we bear the ark of the liberties of the world…. God has given to us, for a future inheritance, the broad domains of the political pagans, that shall yet come and lie down under the shade of our ark, without bloody hands being lifted. God has predestined, mankind expects, great things from our race; and great things we feel in our souls…. Long enough have we been skeptics with regard to ourselves, and doubted whether, indeed, the political Messiah had come. But he has come in us, if we would but give utterance to his promptings. And let us always remember, that with ourselves—almost for the first time in history of earth—national selfishness is unbounded philanthropy; for we cannot do a good to America but we give alms to the world.[3]

While the tragic thread running through *Moby-Dick* may indicate that Melville in his more chastened moments would state these sentiments with a bit more sobriety, this is a breathtaking statement of nationalistic hubris. This, remember, only a decade before the outbreak of America's bloodiest war. The Civil War claimed

---

3. Quoted in Delbanco, 13.

more American lives than both World Wars combined. And it won't do to pretend that these sentiments and the bloody conflict that followed were completely unrelated. No, the kind of blind, romantic hubris that boasts this kind of messianic narcissism is the same kind that butchers brothers, fathers, and sons in the name of democracy, freedom, and equality. And this brings us back to Jonah and the nature of tragedy. Jonah too struggled with a romantic and nationalistic hubris. Israel was God's chosen nation! And yet she was beset by enemies round about, the greatest threat being the rising empire of Assyria, whose capital city was Nineveh. And the Lord sent Jonah there. Jonah wanted the Lord to be merciful to Israel and harsh with Assyria. This is what romanticism does. It wants to cover over sin and evil; it wants to play the victim. But God is a God of truth and love. God's way of saving Israel would be through saving Assyria.

Now, these similarities between Jonah's struggle with God and the romanticism of *Moby-Dick* also bring their differences into high relief. While we might note that there is a superficial similarity in the endings of both stories: a man floating on a coffin in the middle of the ocean and a man sitting alone and dejected on a hillside outside perhaps the largest city in the world at the time—the stories are nevertheless worlds apart.

While Jonah has an open-ended last chapter, it is no tragedy. While Jonah perhaps hoped for death in the sea and certainly prayed for death after God spared the

Assyrians, God refused him in His mercy. And this high-lights perhaps one of the more intriguing elements of the story of Jonah, and that is the clear impression woven through the entire narrative that *God really loves Jonah*. Jonah is hardheaded, but the same compassion that God has for Nineveh, He clearly has for Jonah, and by extension for Israel as a whole.

Tragedy reaches back into the plays of the Greeks in which the lives of men and women were spun by blind fates and fickle gods. No amount of struggle could thwart the prophesied destinies, and the Greeks watched story after story of the same, slow, aching entropy—like watching a predator in nature stalk, stun, and ultimately consume its prey. *Moby-Dick* is no different. From the opening lines in which Ishmael finds himself "involuntarily pausing before coffin warehouses" (1) to the final lines in which Ishmael finds himself floating on an empty ocean supported by that "coffin life-buoy" (680), death and defeat looms over all.

Only the most naïve and inattentive are surprised by the ending of *Moby-Dick*. The novel is not a story that rests on surprise; to the contrary, most of the "glory" of the story resides in that tragic sense of inescapability. As Ahab explains to Starbuck the night before the great chase begins,

> "What is it, what nameless, inscrutable, unearthly
> thing is it; what cozening, hidden lord and master,
> and cruel, remorseless emperor commands me; that
> against all natural lovings and longing, I so keep

> pushing and crowding, and jamming myself on all
> the time; recklessly making me ready to do what in
> my own proper, natural heart, I durst not so much as
> dare?.... By heaven, man, we are turned round and
> round in this world, like yonder windlass, and Fate is
> the handspike" (634-5).

The irony of this sense of tragic fate pushing, crowding, jamming man to some reckless, horrific end in a largely "Christian" culture is just how much distortion and sleight of hand is taking place. Ahab is lying! On the one hand, he says man is majestic and glorious and divine, but on the other hand, he says there is this invisible Fate driving Ahab and his entire crew to their terrible, ugly doom. Which is it? Neither. The only democratic "glory" in man is his fallen nature in sin and the death sentence that rests over everyone. And this sinful nature willfully rebels by suppressing the truth. It must not, at all costs, reckon with thinking in a straight line about what may be true and what may be false.

Becoming a fool while claiming to be wise is hard work, you know, and it means that you must blame God, the world, Fate, chance, whatever, but man must remain innocent, an innocent victim of this "cruel, remorseless emperor." It's all rather laughable if it weren't so pitiful. Melville pouts and sputters and frumps and pretends that he has a very deep point, a real gripe, a real complaint. But the part he left out is the part that Jonah wrote in. It's the part about God ruling over all things with an enormous smile on His face. And if this were real life, the moment the *Pe-quod* went down, those men would have come face to face with that Almighty and Ever-joyful God.

We, like Melville, are industrious and creative in our rebellion. We will catalogue the parts of the whale. We will describe his legends, his uses, his skeleton, his oil. We will diagram our rebellion, our monstrous demons, our obsessions, our lusts, and then it will consume us in the end. And we will try to claim that it was all very beautiful, all very deep and meaningful and dramatic, as we float on our coffin-buoy in the middle of nowhere. *Look, I'm the hero*, we try to claim. No, you're a fool.

There is another captain, the Lord Jesus Christ, who commands the Great Ark of Christendom. He too is a whaler, a sea-serpent hunter. But He is not drunk with vengeance, though He does walk with a limp from an injury inflicted by the great sea dragon to his heel. But the Lord Jesus pierced that fleeing serpent, and now He enjoins all men and women to join his crew.

There is a haunting beauty wound through the world, and it is fierce and terrible. And death surely comes to all. There really are enormous monsters that live in the depths of the sea. But God made them, and God plays with them. And the simple truth necessary to walk fearlessly and boldly in this magical universe is the fact that we have rebelled.

We have sinned, and we have exchanged the glory of God for cheap knockoffs. We are not tragic heroes in our own personal epics. We are all just a bunch of foolish Pips who have lost our minds out at sea. But if we will have the courage and honesty to acknowledge that the only cruel, remorseless emperor that drives us is the mad Ahab residing in every one of our hearts who needs to be drowned in the depths of the sea—and if we surrender to this truth, to the Good Captain, Christ will save us and raise us up to newness of life.

QUOTABLES

1. "Call me Ishmael. Some years ago—never mind how long precisely—having little or no money in my purse, and nothing particular to interest me on shore, I thought I would sail about a little and see the watery part of the world. It is a way I have of driving off the spleen, and regulating the circulation. Whenever I find myself growing grim about the mouth; whenever it is a damp drizzly November in my soul … then, I account it high time to get to sea as soon as I can."

   ~Ishmael, Chapter 1 (p. 1)

2. "[T]he pulpit is ever this earth's foremost part; all the rest comes in its rear; the pulpit leads the world…. Yes, the world's a ship on its passage out, and not a voyage complete; and the pulpit is its prow."

   ~Narrator, Chapter 8 (p. 45)

3. "All visible objects, man, are but as pasteboard masks.
   But in each event—in the living act, the undoubted
   deed—there, some unknown but still reasoning thing
   puts forth the mouldings of its features from behind
   the unreasoning mask. If man will strike, strike through
   the mask! How can the prisoner reach outside except
   by thrusting through the wall? To me, the white whale
   is the wall, shoved near to me. Sometimes I think
   there's naught beyond. But 'tis enough. He tasks me;
   he heaps me; I see in him outrageous strength, with an
   inscrutable malice sinewing it. That inscrutable thing is
   chiefly what I hate; and be the white whale agent, or be
   the white whale principal, I will wreak that hate upon
   him. Talk not to me of blasphemy, man; I'd strike the
   sun if it insulted me."

   ~Captain Ahab, Chapter 36 (pp. 191-192)

4. "Ahab is forever Ahab, man. This whole act's immuta-
   bly decreed. 'Twas rehearsed by thee and me a billion
   years before this ocean rolled. Fool! I am the Fates'
   lieutenant; I act under orders."

   ~Captain Ahab, Chapter 134 (p. 655)

21 SIGNIFICANT
QUESTIONS AND ANSWERS

1. Who was Ishmael in the Bible? Can you think of any
   reasons the narrator might have that name?

   > Ishmael was the son of Hagar (Sarah's maidservant)
   > by Abraham (Gen. 16). He was not the promised
   > seed and so was sent out from Abraham's family,
   > but God still looked out for him (Gen. 21:8-21).
   > Ishmael is generally believed to be the father of the
   > Arab peoples. Perhaps Ishmael the sailor represents
   > this sense of feeling out of place, displaced, rejected,
   > in exile, not a son of the promise—and yet, perhaps
   > some hint of God's care still being on him, though
   > lost and far from home.

2. Describe the friendship that develops between Ishmael
   and Queequeg. What significance does that seem to
   have for the rest of the story?

At first, Ishmael is very wary of Queequeg the
head-peddling, tattooed cannibal. The first night
they spend together as bedmates is pretty humorous
and awkward. Yet, Ishmael warms up to Queequeg,
even to the point of joining him in some of his pagan
rituals. This friendship seems to be a significant un-
dercurrent for the entire book, where the wildness of
nature or paganism is embraced alongside of certain,
selective Christian virtues.

3. Describe the chapel and Father Mapple's sermon.
What do those chapters indicate about the coming
narrative?

The chapel is a standing memorial to many sailors
lost at sea. Father Mapple's sermon is particularly
focused on the story of Jonah and God's determina-
tion to destroy all sin.

4. What does Elijah foretell, and why is it significant that
his name is "Elijah?"

Elijah foretells the destruction of the *Pequod* and all
aboard it. Elijah was the famous Hebrew prophet
who confronted the wicked Israelite King Ahab.

5. Describe Captain Ahab. Why is he named "Ahab"?

Ahab is an old, grizzled sea captain who is fif-
ty-eight years old. He is at turns obsessive and
merciless, and yet at other moments circumspect,
surprisingly aware of himself and others, and even

momentarily tender. Ultimately, he claims to be
under the power of "Fate" and unable not to seek
revenge on the white whale, Moby Dick.

6. Name and describe the four harpooners. What do they
   seem to represent in *Moby-Dick*?

   Queequeg is a tattooed, cannibal, island prince and
   the harpooner in Starbuck's boat. Tashtego is an
   Indian from Gay Head in Martha's Vineyard and
   is the harpooner in Stub's boat. Daggoo is a giant
   black man, an African "savage" standing at six foot
   five inches with two golden hoops in his ears, and
   he is the harpooner for Flask. Fedallah is the old,
   white-turbaned, middle-eastern or Asian harpooner
   in Ahab's personal boat. The harpooners seem to
   represent something of the natural goodness of man
   in nature. All four are strong, cunning, courageous,
   and thoroughly pagan or non-Christian.

7. What does the author want us to think about whales
   and whaling?

   Melville presents whales as exotic, wonderful crea-
   tures full of "treasure"—resources for the good of
   man; whaling is a glorious venture, truly dangerous,
   terrifying, and yet heroic.

8. Describe the process of hunting and killing a whale.

   The men on watch cry out "thar she blows!" The
   whaling boats are lowered with their respective

crews and begin rowing toward the whales. When
the whale breeches, the harpooner lets his weapon
fly, piercing into the whale. Then the line is man-
aged as the whale drags the boat through the sea.
Whenever the whale slows, the line is hauled in
further until the whale can go no further, and then
dart after dart and is sent into the animal until it
dies.

9.   Where is God in *Moby-Dick*?

God is everywhere and nowhere. There are many,
many allusions implicit and explicit to the God of
the Bible, Scripture, and Christian tradition, but
there is really no truly evangelical apprehension of
God as He truly is in Scripture and in the gospel of
Jesus Christ.

10. What are some possible meanings of the White Whale
itself, Moby Dick?

The whale may represent the powers of nature,
death, God, fate, gods, demons, human nature, the
self of man, and history.

11. Why would the first ship the *Pequod* meets be called
the *Jeroboam*? Who was Jeroboam in the Bible? What
might the significance of that be?

Jeroboam was the first king of the northern kingdom of Israel after the kingdom divided between
north and south after the death of Solomon.

Jeroboam was offered God's blessing, but set up
gold calves to worship in the north out of fear that
Israel would return to Judah if they continued to
worship God in Jerusalem. In this way Jeroboam
the king rejected God's offer to be blessed through
obedience. The *Jeroboam* ship likely represents the
opportunity for blessing and success rejected.

12. What sort of vision for manhood and masculinity (and
by implication femininity) does *Moby-Dick* present?

The vision of masculinity in *Moby-Dick* is wholly
absent of women. The feminine largely emerges
in the symbolism of nature and the ocean. In this
sense, men "find their masculinity" all alone or only
amongst the camaraderie and friendship of other
men. Masculinity is largely presented as courage,
(male) friendship, overcoming internal and external
difficulties, fears, and dangers. Masculinity is pic-
tured as contemplation of beauty (of creation) and
philosophy alongside the warfare of hunting whales.

13. Compare and contrast the masculinity of *Moby-Dick*
with the masculinity of the Bible.

Beginning in the Garden of Eden, the Bible says
that it is not good for a man to be alone and creates
a woman to be the first man's companion, assistant,
and lover. This is a striking contrast to *Moby-Dick*.
God does give man the task of taking dominion of
all creation, and that includes the great fish of the
deep, but that task is given to both the man and the

woman together. The Bible says that it is not good
for man to be alone, and that woman is the glory
of man. Fatherhood and motherhood and family
and church community are central to embracing
biblical masculinity. There is a sense in which a man
is *less* masculine alone or only with other men. As
a woman embraces her glory, she shines on man
glorifying him as a man. *Moby-Dick* seems to imply
that a man must find himself alone or with other
men, and women and children only come into that
task incidentally.

14. What are the central conflicts in the story? List at least
five.

The conflict between Ahab and Moby Dick,
between Ahab and himself, between Ahab and the
chief mates, between Ishmael and himself, and most
broadly, between man and nature, or man and God.

15. What is the significance of the stage directions and play-
like formatting in various chapters?

Given Ahab's statements about being players in a
drama rehearsed millions of years before creation,
Melville seems to be playing with the idea that
"fate" is driving everything. This is also a "play" on
the classical tragedy tradition, which was often
presented as a drama "on stage." This is also a nod to
Shakespeare, who often did the same.

16. Can you point to several elements in the story that indicate that *Moby-Dick* belongs in the Romantic genre of literature?

> *Moby-Dick* belongs in the Romantic genre because of its transcendent and epic subject matter, its fundamental appeal to sentiments and feelings, and its celebration of human life, human accomplishment, and human frailty.

17. Why is Romanticism ultimately a worldview of despair?

> Romanticism is ultimately a worldview of despair because it has no true salvation. The only "salvation" it offers is heroic feelings in the face of disappointment, failure, and ultimately death. But all the warmest feelings in the world cannot undo the true predicament of fallen humanity and the curse of sin.

18. What has happened to the *Rachel* and what does this episode demonstrate about Ahab?

> The *Rachel* lost one of its whaling boats, and the captain's own son was aboard it. Ahab refuses to help the heartbroken captain in any way. The episode demonstrates Ahab's cruelty and obsession in the face of human suffering.

19. What are the most significant influences on Melville's
    writing in *Moby-Dick*? Can you give examples of each?

    The Bible, Shakespeare, classical Greek (tragic)
    literature and dramas. Examples will vary.

20. What role and significance does the biblical story of
    Jonah play either explicitly or implicitly throughout the
    novel?

    Beginning with Father Mapple's sermon, includ-
    ing one explicit chapter on the story of Jonah, the
    entire novel implicitly plays behind the scenes as
    a significant theme. The story of Jonah is all about
    one man's fight against God, against His justice,
    against His way of running history, and though
    Melville tells his story significantly differently
    (the survivor is not repentant), many of the same
    themes and dynamics are at work.

21. Describe Starbuck, Stubb, and Flask and what their
    characters mean in the story.

    The chief mates seem to largely stand for western
    sanity. They object to Ahab's insane and obsessive
    mission, but they are still drawn to the glory of
    whaling. They give voice to many of our most com-
    mon objections as readers and members of western
    culture. But if the story of *Moby-Dick* is to be taken
    seriously, Melville seems to indicate that our true
    glory is found in embracing the wilder natures of
    the pagans.

FURTHER DISCUSSION
AND REVIEW

Master what you have read by reviewing and integrating the different elements of this classic.

SETTING AND CHARACTERS
Be able to compare and contrast the personalities (including strengths, weaknesses, and mannerisms) of each character. Which characters change over the course of the novel? Which do not?

PLOT
Be able to describe the beginning, middle, and end of the book along with specific details that move the plot forward and make it compelling.

CONFLICT
Go through the character list and describe the tension between any and all main characters. Then, think about

whether any characters have internal conflict (in their own minds). Is there any overt conflict (fighting), or conflict with impersonal forces?

THEME STATEMENTS

Be able to describe what this classic is telling us about the world. Is the message true? What truth can we take from the plot, characters, conflict, and themes (even if the author didn't believe that truth)? Do any objects take on added meaning because of repetition or their place in the story (i.e., do any objects become symbols)? How does the author use perspective, tone, and irony to tell the truth?

> "The greatness of man lies in his decision to be stronger than his condition" (Albert Camus). Consider some of the different ways that Melville displays the greatness of man, perhaps even in defiance of the universe.

> Does man have a preordained destiny? Are all his actions futile? How does Melville's romanticism leave him stuck with fate and death?

> What does it mean to be a man? How is the vision of manhood in this novel superior to what we see in our culture, and where does it fall short? Why are there no women, and what do you think this tells us about Melville?

A NOTE FROM THE PUBLISHER:
TAKING THE CLASSICS QUIZ

Once you have finished the worldview guide, you can prepare for the end-of-book test. Each test will consist of a short-answer section on the book itself and the author, a short-answer section on plot and the narrative, and a long-answer essay section on worldview, conflict, and themes.

Each quiz, along with other helps, can be downloaded for free at www.canonpress.com/ClassicsQuizzes. If you have any questions about the quiz or its answers or the Worldview Guides in general, you can contact Canon Press at service@canonpress.com or 208.892.8074.

ABOUT THE AUTHOR

Toby J. Sumpter is pastor of Trinity Reformed Church and author of *Blood-Bought World: Jesus, Idols, and the Bible* and the commentary *Job Through New Eyes: A Son for Glory*. He and his wife Jenny live in Moscow, Idaho with their four children. Toby is also a host of the weekly CrossPolitic Show and Podcast.